Contents • Inhalt • Table des matières

Orchestration • Besetzung

PART 1	Solo in C	Flute, Oboe or Violin
PART 1	Solo in B♭	Clarinet
PART 1	Solo in E♭	Alto Saxophone
PART 2	in C	Flute, Oboe or Violin
PART 2	in B♭	Clarinet
PART 2	in E♭	Alto Saxophone
PART 3	in C	Violin
PART 3	in B♭	Clarinet
PART 3	in B♭	Tenor Saxophone
PART 3		Viola
PART 3	in F	French Horn
PART 4	in C	Cello, Double Bass or Bassoon
PART 4	in B♭	Bass Clarinet

PIANO (optional) for rehearsal or to support the performance

Mack the Knife

(from The Threepenny Opera)

Kurt Weill
(1900–1950)
arr. James Rae

Universal Edition UE 21 266

UE
Universal Edition

centrestage 2

Four-part flexible chamber music arrangements featuring a soloist

Mack the Knife

(The Threepenny Opera)

by KURT WEILL

Habanera

(Carmen)

by GEORGES BIZET

Arranged by James Rae

www.universaledition.com
vienna · london · new york

UE 21 266
ISMN M-008-07551-3
UPC 8-03452-02283-1
ISBN 978-3-7024-2742-9

Preface

Centre Stage is a series of elementary chamber music arrangements for flexible ensemble which feature a soloist. The pieces are scored in four parts with an optional supporting piano accompaniment.

The study of chamber music is essential for the musical development of any serious student as it encourages careful listening, builds confidence and most importantly, is great fun to play.

These arrangements make ideal concert items and are also suitable for music festivals.

●

Vorwort

Centre Stage ist eine Reihe von einfachen Kammermusikarrangements für flexible Ensemblekombinationen mit einem Solisten. Die Stücke wurden für vier Stimmen und einer je nach Bedarf einsetzbaren, unterstützenden Klavierbegleitung geschrieben.

Das Studium von Kammermusik ist für jeden ernsthaften Musikschüler unentbehrlich, da es zum aufmerksamen Zuhören anhält, das Selbstvertrauen stärkt und, was am wichtigsten ist, Spaß beim Spielen macht.

Die Stücke eignen sich ideal zum Konzertvortrag und passen auch gut in Musikfestivals.

●

Préface

Centre Stage est une série d'arrangements de musique de chambre de niveau élémentaire destinés à une formation de composition flexible comprenant un soliste. Ils sont instrumentés à quatre parties soutenues par un accompagnement de piano facultatif.

La pratique de la musique de chambre est essentielle au développement musical de tout étudiant sérieux. Elle favorise l'écoute attentive, renforce l'assurance et, surtout, procure beaucoup de plaisir.

Ces morceaux constituent des pièces de concert idéales et conviennent à toutes les festivités musicales.

Habanera
(from Carmen)

Georges Bizet
(1838–1875)
arr. James Rae

Universal Edition UE 21 266

Children on Stage

Each volume contains parts for C and B♭ instruments, piano and optional bass and percussion. For lower to middle grade players. Also contains a synopsis and ideas for staging as a dance or dramatic production.

UE 30 303
THE CARNIVAL OF THE ANIMALS Saint-Saëns

UE 30 304
PEER GYNT Grieg

UE 30 305
GOSPELS AND SPIRITUALS Traditional

UE 30 306
A MUSICAL SLEIGH RIDE Mozart

UE 30 307
THE MAGIC FLUTE Mozart

UE 30 308
A CHRISTMAS CONCERT Bruckner

UE 30 309
HANSEL AND GRETEL Humperdinck

UE 30 310
THE CUNNING LITTLE VIXEN Janáček

UE 30 311
THE NUTCRACKER Tchaikovsky

UE 30 312
A MIDSUMMER NIGHT'S DREAM Mendelssohn

UE 30 313
CHILDREN'S CORNER Debussy

Chamberpops

For middle grade players. Each contains two pieces for woodwind and/or saxophone ensemble with optional rhythm section or bassoon arranged in popular styles.

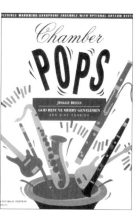

UE 16 518
THE LASS OF RICHMOND HILL *Arr.* Mike Cornick
FRERE JACQUES *Arr.* James Rae

UE 16 557
MEN OF HARLECH *Arr.* James Rae
THE BLAYDON RACES *Arr.* James Rae

UE 19 213
JINGLE BELLS *Arr.* Mike Cornick
GOD REST YE MERRY GENTLEMEN *Arr.* Mike Cornick

Mack the Knife
(from The Threepenny Opera)

Piano

Kurt Weill
(1900–1950)
arr. James Rae

Universal Edition UE 21 266n

Piano

Habanera
(from Carmen)

Georges Bizet
(1838–1875)
arr. James Rae

Allegretto quasi Andantino ♩ = 72

Universal Edition UE 21 266n

Mack the Knife

(from The Threepenny Opera)

Kurt Weill
(1900–1950)
arr. James Rae

Universal Edition UE 21 266m

Part 4
Bass Clarinet in B♭

Habanera

(from Carmen)

Georges Bizet
(1838–1875)
arr. James Rae

Universal Edition UE 21 266m

Part 4
in C (Cello, Double Bass
or Bassoon)

Mack the Knife

(from The Threepenny Opera)

Kurt Weill
(1900–1950)
arr. James Rae

Universal Edition UE 21 2661

Part 4
in C (Cello, Double Bass
or Bassoon)

Habanera

(from Carmen)

Georges Bizet
(1838 – 1875)
arr. James Rae

Allegretto quasi Andantino ♩ = 72

pizz. (for cello and double bass)

Universal Edition UE 21 2661

Part 3
Horn in F

Mack the Knife

(from The Threepenny Opera)

Kurt Weill
(1900–1950)
arr. James Rae

Universal Edition UE 21 266k

Part 3
Horn in F

Habanera
(from Carmen)

Georges Bizet
(1838–1875)
arr. James Rae

Universal Edition UE 21 266k

Mack the Knife

(from The Threepenny Opera)

Kurt Weill
(1900–1950)
arr. James Rae

Universal Edition UE 21 266j

Habanera

(from Carmen)

Georges Bizet
(1838–1875)
arr. James Rae

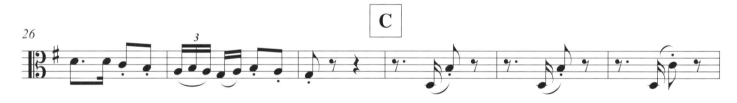

Universal Edition UE 21 266j

Mack the Knife

(from The Threepenny Opera)

Kurt Weill
(1900–1950)
arr. James Rae

Universal Edition UE 21 266i

Habanera

(from Carmen)

Georges Bizet
(1838–1875)
arr. James Rae

Universal Edition UE 21 266i

Part 3
B♭ Clarinet

Mack the Knife

(from The Threepenny Opera)

Kurt Weill
(1900–1950)
arr. James Rae

Universal Edition UE 21 266h

Habanera

(from Carmen)

Georges Bizet
(1838–1875)
arr. James Rae

Universal Edition UE 21 266h

Part 3
in C (Violin)

Mack the Knife

(from The Threepenny Opera)

Kurt Weill
(1900–1950)
arr. James Rae

Universal Edition UE 21 266g

Part 3
in C (Violin)

Habanera

(from Carmen)

Georges Bizet
(1838–1875)
arr. James Rae

Allegretto quasi Andantino ♩ = 72

Universal Edition UE 21 266g

Mack the Knife

(from The Threepenny Opera)

Kurt Weill
(1900–1950)
arr. James Rae

Universal Edition UE 21 266f

Habanera

(from Carmen)

Georges Bizet
(1838–1875)
arr. James Rae

Allegretto quasi Andantino ♩ = 72

Universal Edition UE 21 266f

Part 2
B♭ Clarinet

Mack the Knife

(from The Threepenny Opera)

Kurt Weill
(1900–1950)
arr. James Rae

Universal Edition UE 21 266e

Habanera

(from Carmen)

Georges Bizet
(1838–1875)
arr. James Rae

Universal Edition UE 21 266e

Part 2
in C (Flute, Oboe or Violin)

Mack the Knife
(from The Threepenny Opera)

Kurt Weill
(1900 – 1950)
arr. James Rae

Universal Edition UE 21 266d

Part 2
in C (Flute, Oboe or Violin)

Habanera

(from Carmen)

Georges Bizet
(1838–1875)
arr. James Rae

*) Small notes for flute and oboe

Universal Edition UE 21 266d

Part 1 Solo
E♭ Alto Saxophone

Mack the Knife
(from The Threepenny Opera)

Kurt Weill
(1900–1950)
arr. James Rae

This arrangement © 2005 by European American Music Corporation
All Rights outside of the United States, Great Britain and the British
reversionary territories controlled by Universal Edition A.G., Vienna

Universal Edition UE 21 266c

Habanera

(from Carmen)

Georges Bizet
(1838–1875)
arr. James Rae

Universal Edition UE 21 266c

Part 1 Solo
Bb Clarinet

Mack the Knife

(from The Threepenny Opera)

Kurt Weill
(1900 – 1950)
arr. James Rae

Universal Edition UE 21 266b

Habanera

(from Carmen)

Georges Bizet
(1838–1875)
arr. James Rae

Universal Edition UE 21 266b

Mack the Knife

(from The Threepenny Opera)

Kurt Weill
(1900–1950)
arr. James Rae

Universal Edition UE 21 266a

Part 1 Solo
in C (Flute, Oboe or Violin)

Habanera
(from Carmen)

Georges Bizet
(1838–1875)
arr. James Rae

Allegretto quasi Andantino ♩ = 72

Universal Edition UE 21 266a